I0002883

About the Author

Mr. Paul Watson has many years of experience working in large software projects. He has worked on large investment banking projects in tier-1 Software Companies in USA, Australia and Switzerland.

His hobbies include travelling, watching football and learning latest technological stuff.

Who is this book for

This book is for software professionals who want to learn Bamboo. Book contains examples on how to integrate various technology stack with Bamboo. This book covers all basic as well as advanced concepts in Bamboo. This book will be useful for software developers, testers as well as Dev Ops to understand the Bamboo Ecosystem.

Book covers popular build management tools like Maven and Gradle. It also includes how to create a deployment project for a web based application using Tomcat.

What is covered in this book

This book covers below topics on Bamboo.

1. Introduction
2. Installation
3. Creating projects and plans
4. Cloning (Copying) a build plan
5. Configuring visible projects in Bamboo
6. Configuring the build plan
7. Java project
8. Visual Studio .Net Project tasks
9. Command line builds in Bamboo
10. Running the build plans manually
11. Viewing the build history and build logs
12. Bamboo Reports
13. Authors Page in Bamboo
14. Executing Selenium tests in Bamboo
15. Creating and viewing artifacts
16. Running customized build plan
17. Build queue in Bamboo
18. Bamboo Administration
19. Adding deployment project to build plan in Bamboo
20. Web application deployment to tomcat using Bamboo

Table of Contents

1. Introduction

Bamboo is one of the most popular CI server by the company -
Atlassian(https://www.atlassian.com/software/bamboo).

Key features of Bamboo are given below.

1. It supports various version control systems like bitbucket, cvs, subversion, git, perforcem and mercurial.
2. Supports all important tasks like ant, maven, gradle, make tasks, tomcat, SSH, Linux and windows commands, SCP task, PHPUnit, Nunit, Node, MSTest, MSBuild, Grunt, Grails, AWS codeDeploy
3. It also supports the deployment projects.
4. A build plan has one or more stages. **Each stage has one or more jobs**. Each job can have one or multiple tasks like maven or gradle etc. Jobs in a single stage can run simultaneously but stages and tasks within a job run in sequence only.

2. Installation

In this topic, you will learn how to download and install Bamboo.

Get your Bamboo evaluation version from **Atlassian website** (https://www.atlassian.com/software/bamboo/download) I downloaded zip version of bamboo as shown in below image.

Try Bamboo free for 30 days

 Mac OS X   Windows   Linux

Bamboo 5.12.1 - Windows Installer, 64-bit
208.8 MB • Released 26-May-2016 (Release notes | Upgrade notes)

Bamboo 5.12.1 - Windows Installer, 32-bit
208.4 MB • Released 26-May-2016 (Release notes | Upgrade notes)

Bamboo 5.12.1 - ZIP Archive
206.6 MB • Released 26-May-2016 (Release notes | Upgrade notes)

Zip version of Bamboo

Then I extracted the zip folder using 7Zip utility.

After that I added a bamboo home directory in the file -
C:\Users\Sagar\Downloads\atlassian-bamboo-
5.12.1\atlassian-bamboo\WEB-INF\classes\bamboo-
init.properties

bamboo.home=C:\Users\Sagar\bamboo-home

Then I modified the ports of Bamboo. By default Bamboo
is accessible from 8085 port but we can change it from
below file.

C:\Users\Sagar\Downloads\atlassian-bamboo-
5.12.1\conf\server.xml

```
<Server port="9998" shutdown="SHUTDOWN">

    <!--APR library loader. Documentation at /docs/apr.html -->
    <Listener className="org.apache.catalina.core.AprLifecycleListener" SSLEngine="on"/>
    <!-- JMX Support for the Tomcat server. Documentation at /docs/non-existent.html -->
    <Listener className="org.apache.catalina.mbeans.GlobalResourcesLifecycleListener"/>

]   <!-- Global JNDI resources
         Documentation at /docs/jndi-resources-howto.html
    -->

]   <!-- A "Service" is a collection of one or more "Connectors" that share
         a single "Container" Note: A "Service" is not itself a "Container",
         so you may not define subcomponents such as "Valves" at this level.
         Documentation at /docs/config/service.html
    -->
]   <Service name="Catalina">

    <Connector
        protocol="HTTP/1.1"
        port="9999"

        maxThreads="150" minSpareThreads="25"
        connectionTimeout="20000"
        disableUploadTimeout="true"
        acceptCount="100"
```

Bamboo ports

After that We can start the server by executing below command.

```
C:\Users\Sagar\Downloads\atlassian-bamboo-5.12.1>bin\start-bamboo.bat

To run Bamboo in the foreground, start the server with start-bamboo.bat /fg

Bamboo Server Edition
    Version : 5.12.1

JAVA_HOME "C:\Program Files\Java\jdk1.8.0_77" contains spaces. Please change to a location without spaces
 problems.

If you encounter issues starting or stopping Bamboo Server, please see the Troubleshooting guide at https:
tlassian.com/display/BAMBOO/Installing+Bamboo+on+Windows

Using CATALINA_BASE:   "C:\Users\Sagar\Downloads\atlassian-bamboo-5.12.1"
Using CATALINA_HOME:   "C:\Users\Sagar\Downloads\atlassian-bamboo-5.12.1"
Using CATALINA_TMPDIR: "C:\Users\Sagar\Downloads\atlassian-bamboo-5.12.1\temp"
Using JRE_HOME:        "C:\Program Files\Java\jdk1.8.0_77\jre"
Using CLASSPATH:       "C:\Users\Sagar\Downloads\atlassian-bamboo-5.12.1\bin\bootstrap.jar;C:\Users\Sagar\[
ssian-bamboo-5.12.1\bin\tomcat-juli.jar"
```

Start Bamboo server using command prompt

Then We can access the Bamboo at
url http://localhost:9999

First time, you will to get license key from Bamboo. To get the license key, click on contact Atlassian link which will take you to license page. Once the license Key provided, you can click on express installation and then create an admin account.

Welcome to Atlassian Bamboo continuous integration server!

Please enter your license information and choose a setup method below to complete the installation of Bamboo.

Enter your license

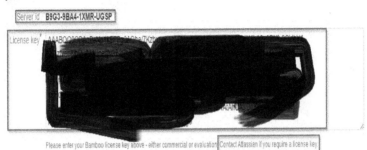

Please enter your Bamboo license key above - either commercial or evaluation. Contact Atlassian if you require a license key.

Select setup method

Express installation

Installs Bamboo with default settings and an embedded database.
Recommended if you are evaluating or demonstrating Bamboo, as it will get you up and running as

Express installation

Bamboo license set up

Bamboo – express installation

Set up administrator user

Please enter the details of the administrator user for this installation of Bamboo.

Username*	sagar
Password*	••••••••
Confirm password*	••••••••
Full name*	Salunke
Email*	sagar@softpost.org

Finish

Create admin account on Bamboo

If everything goes fine, you will be taken to the Bamboo home page.

⚙Bamboo   My Bamboo   Build ▾   Deploy ▾   Create ▾

Build Dashboard

Let's get building!

Now that the installation and the set
it's time to create your first build plar

Build plans hold all the instructions t
your software. Whenever you make
Bamboo triggers your build plan anc

Create your first build plan

Build dashboard - Bamboo Home page

3. Creating projects and plans

Here is the list of steps to create new project and build plan in Bamboo.

1. Click on create a new plan
2. Select new project from the project drop down
3. Provide the project name and build plan name
4. Link the VCS repository to build plan
5. Add extra tasks to the default job if you want. But it is optional
6. Enable plan and click on create button
7. New project and build plan will be displayed on Bamboo dashboard.

Below images show how to create new build plan and project in Bamboo.

Project	Plan	Build	Completed
⌄ Maven Project	MavenBuild	ⓘ #1	51 minutes ago
	Testng	⊘ #1	46 minutes ago

2 of 2 plans shown

Creating new build plan in Bamboo

Create a new plan

Configure plan

How to create a build plan

Your build plan defines everything about your build process. Each plan has a Default job when it is created. More advanced configuration options (including those for plugins), and the ability to add more jobs will be available to you after creating this plan.

Project and build plan name

Project	New Project

The project the new plan will be created in.

Project name	Visual Studio tests

Project key	VST

Eg. AT (for a project named Atlassian)

Plan name	Visual Studio tests

Plan key	VST

Eg. WEB (for a plan named Website)

Project name and build plan name in Bamboo

Link repository to new build plan

Repository host* ○ Previously linked repository

⦿ Link new repository

GitHub ▾

Display name* | Visual studio repo |

GitHub details

Username* | reply2sagar@gmail.com |

The GitHub user required to access the repositories.

Password | •••••••• |

The password required by the GitHub username.

Repository | reply2sagar/vstestrepo ▾ | Load Repositories

Select the repository you want to use for your Plan.

Branch | master ▾ |

Choose a branch you want to check out your code from.

Linking repository to build plan in Bamboo

Configure tasks

Each plan has a default job when it is created. In this section, you can configure the Tasks for this plan's default job. You can add n once the plan has been created.

A task is an operation that is run on a Bamboo working directory using an executable. An example of task would be the execution command, an Ant Task or a Maven goal. Learn more about tasks.

No task selected

Select a task from the list on the left to configure it.

Enable this plan?

By selecting this option your plan will be available for building and change detection straight away.
do not select this option if you have advanced configuration changes to make after creation.

Create   Cancel

Create a build plan with default checkout task

16

Build plans as shown on dashboard in Bamboo

4. Cloning (Copying) a build plan

Sometimes, it is easier to use build configuration from existing build plan. You can clone or copy existing build plan as shown in below image.

All plan configuration like jobs, tasks, triggers, Repository details, variables are copied as well. You can put new build plan in existing project or new project.

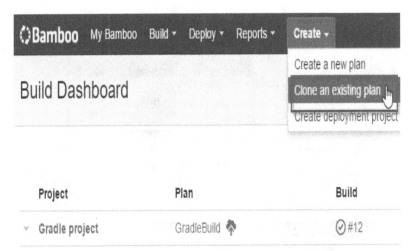

cloning existing build plan in Bamboo

Below image shows that we can put new plan In existing project or new project.

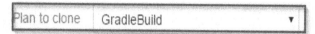

Clone an existing plan

On this page, you can make a copy of a plan and its entire configuration.

Plan to clone

Plan to clone	GradleBuild ▼

This will be used as the template for creating your new plan.

Destination project

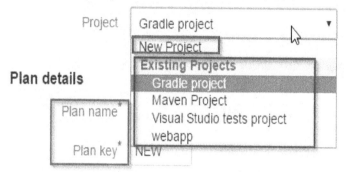

Project | Gradle project ▼

New Project

Existing Projects
Gradle project
Maven Project
Visual Studio tests project
webapp

Plan details

Plan name*

Plan key* NEW

Eg. WEB (for a plan named Website)

Plan description

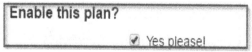

Enable this plan?

☑ Yes please!

Clone existing plan to new or existing project in Bamboo

5. Configuring visible projects

By default, you will see all projects and build plans on Bamboo Dashboard. But we are only interested only the build plans of our project.

You can use filters to view only specific project and build plans on Bamboo Dashboard.

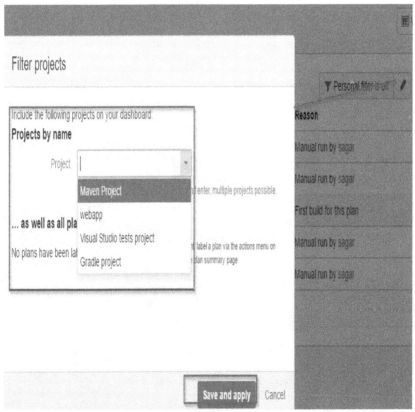

Filtering projects in Bamboo

You can also view only favorite plans by clicking on Wallboard as shown in below image.

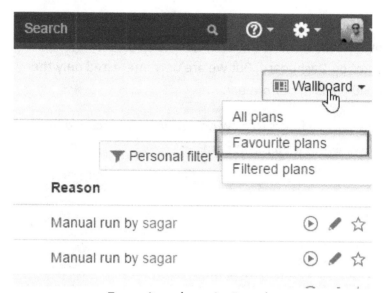

Favorite plans in Bamboo

6. Configuring the build plan

6.1 Editing build plan

You can edit or configure the build plan in 2 ways.

1. By clicking on edit button next to plan on Dashboard page
2. By clicking on build plan and then from actions menu

Below images show how we can edit build plan.

Plan	Build	Completed	Tests	Reason	
GradleBuild	#12	1 week ago	No tests found	Manual run by sagar	
MavenBuild	#3	1 week ago	4 of 17 failed	Manual run by sagar	
Testng	#1	1 week ago	1 passed	First build for this plan	
Visual Studio tests build plan	#5	1 week ago	1 passed	Manual run by sagar	

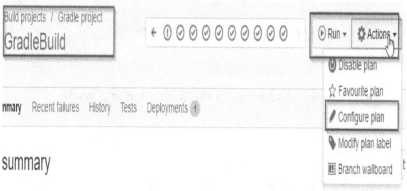

Configure plan from Actions menu

6.2 Changing the plan name

Below image shows how we can edit the Build plan name and project name in Bamboo.

You have to click on edit build plan button and then go to Plan Details tab.

Build projects / Gradle project / GradleBuild

Configuration - GradleBuild

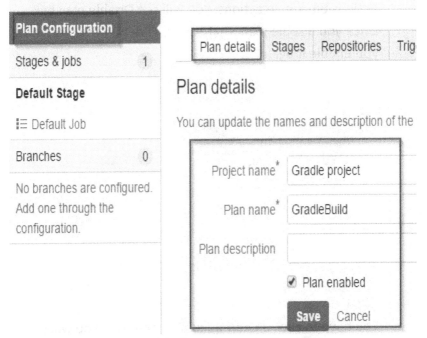

Changing build plan name in Bamboo

6.3 Disable plan

Now let us see how to disable the build plan in Bamboo.

You have to click on edit build plan and then you will see Actions button. In actions, you will see Disable plan link. Once you disable plan, that build will not be triggered until you enable it again.

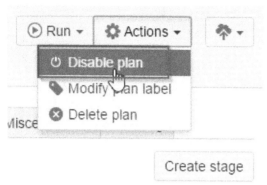

Disable plan in Bamboo

6.4 Delete the build plan

You have to click on edit build plan and then you will see Actions button. In actions, you will see Delete plan link as shown in below image. Once deleted, you will not be able to get it back. So be careful before deleting a build plan.

Delete build plan in Bamboo

6.5 Configuring stages , Jobs and Tasks

Each Bamboo build plan has one or more stages. Stages run in sequence.

Each stage can have one or more jobs. Jobs in a single stage run simultaneously.

Each job in Bamboo has one or more tasks. Task is the smallest unit of work that bamboo does. For example - maven test, gradle, MSBuild etc.

Tasks within a job run in sequence.

Below image explains relationship between stages, jobs and tasks.

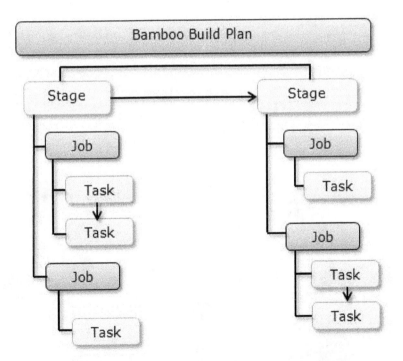

Bamboo build plan - Stages, Jobs and tasks

Below images show how to edit build plan and add new stages, jobs and tasks in Bamboo.

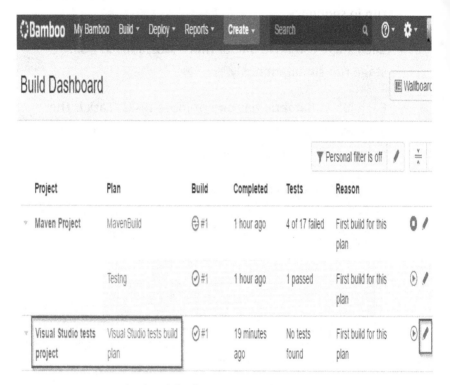

Edit build plan in Bamboo

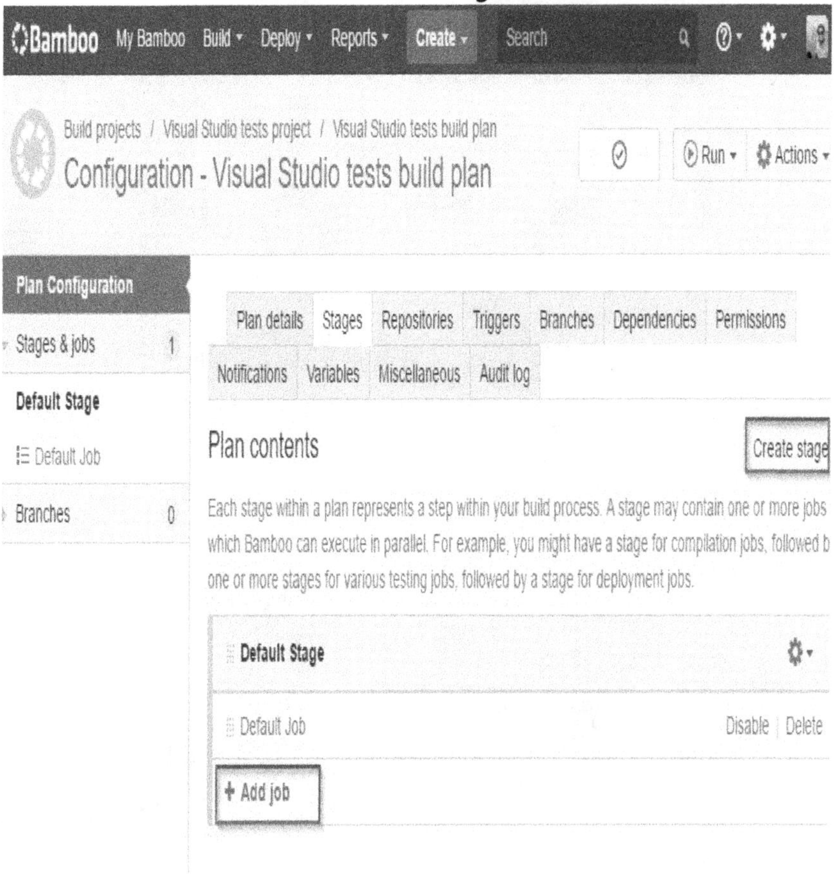

Create new stage and job in Bamboo

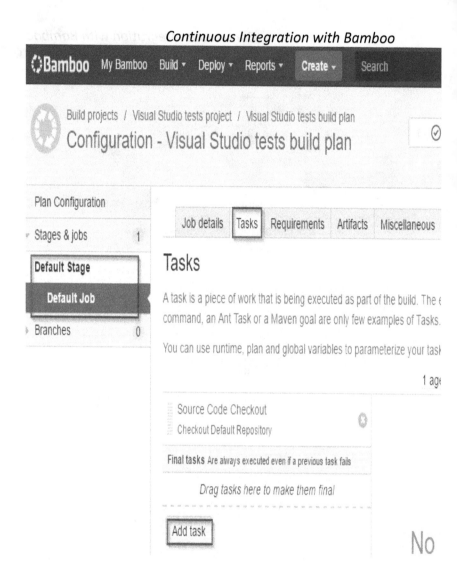

Adding task to Job in Bamboo build plan

6.6 Configuring build plan repositories

You can add or remove the repositories in build plan from Repositories tab on build configuration page.

If some repository is shared among various plans, you can edit it from **linked repositories page**. Below image shows that we have associated one repository (gradlerepo) to the build plan. We can add multiple repositories to the build.

Adding repositories in Bamboo

Below image shows that we have added new repository - repo1. Notice that build plan will use this repository to execute the build because we have ordered it to first position (Default repository).

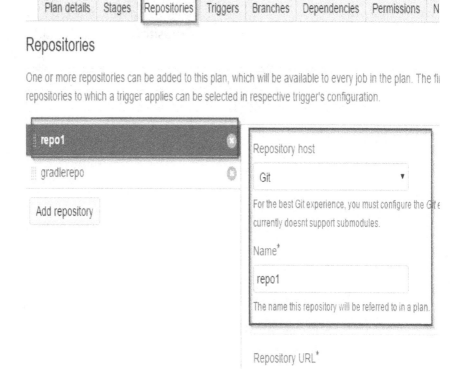

Configuring a default repository

6.7 Adding Scheduled build trigger

Using scheduled build trigger, we can configure builds to run at specific time in a day, week or month.

Below image shows how we can add new trigger in build plan.

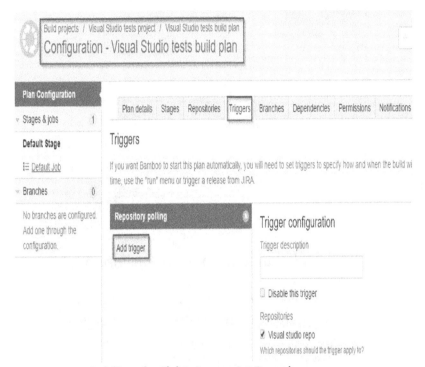

Adding build trigger in Bamboo

Below image shows how to configure the scheduled build in Bamboo.

Triggers

If you want Bamboo to start this plan automatically, you will need to set triggers to specify how and when the build i time, use the "run" menu or trigger a release from JIRA.

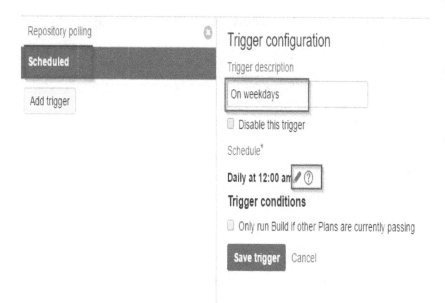

Scheduled trigger configuration

Below image shows how to use schedule editor to specify the time for the build. Notice that we can also give cron expression. Below trigger will allow us to run build on every weekday at 12 a.m.

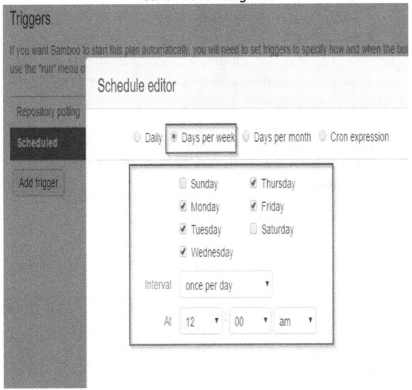

week day scheduled trigger in Bamboo

6.8 Adding Repository polling trigger

Repository polling trigger allows us to run the build when source code in the repository changes. Bamboo polls the repository periodically or at specific time and if there are new changes in the repository, build is triggered.

As shown in below image, Bamboo will poll the Visual studio repository after every 180 seconds. If changes are detected, build is triggered.

Triggers

If you want Bamboo to start this plan automatically, you will need to set triggers to specify how and when the build will be triggered. time, use the "run" menu or trigger a release from JIRA.

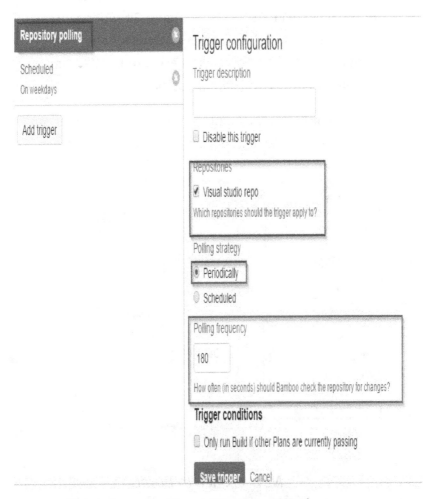

Repository polling trigger in Bamboo

6.9 Adding new branch

If you are using git repository in a build plan, you might want to run the same build on different branches of the same repository. Bamboo allows you to create a branch for the build plan. As you know that a Git repository can have multiple branches. Every Git repository has one default branch. So when build is executed, code from default branch is checked out and build is run.

If you want to run the build on different branch, you can add new branch to your build as shown in below image.

New branch in Bamboo

Below image shows that we have created new branch with name bugfix for our build plan.

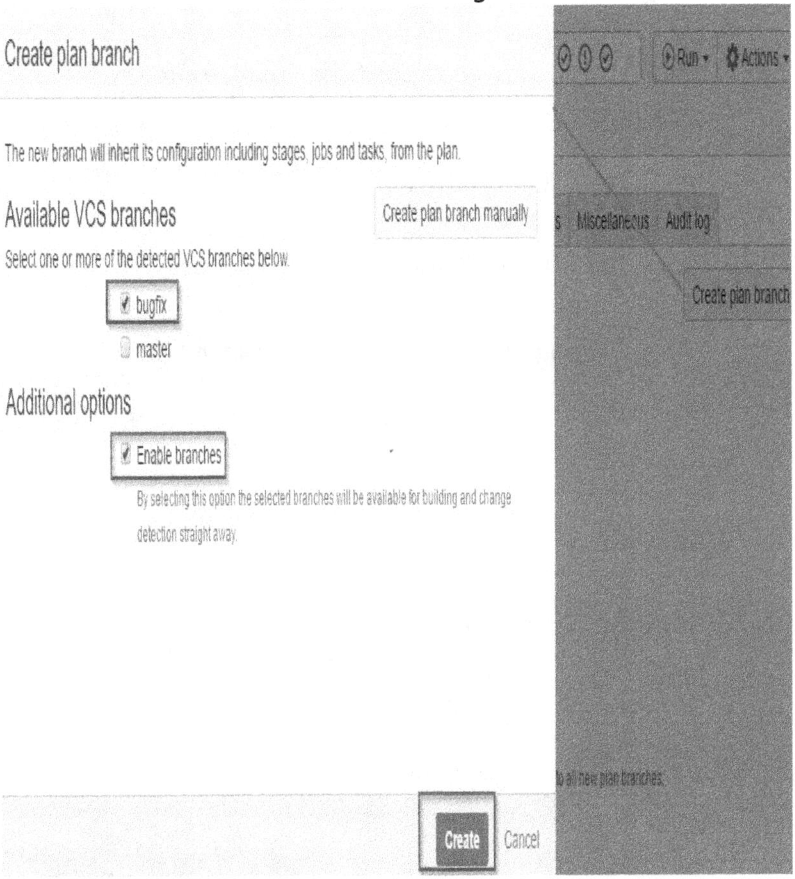

Creating new branch for build plan in Bamboo

6.10 Running a branch

In a build plan using git repository, you can run the build on different branches.

You have to follow below steps to run build on a branch.

1. Open the build plan summary
2. Click on branches tab
3. Click on play icon next to the branch name

Below image shows how to run the build with different branch.

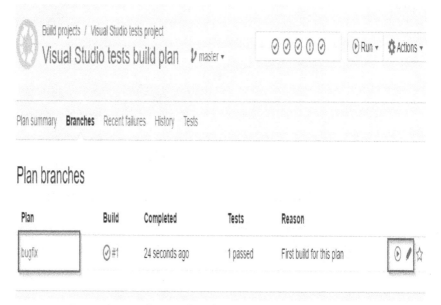

Running a branch of plan in Bamboo

6.11 Branch actions in Bamboo

You can perform below actions on a branch of a build plan in Bamboo.

1. Disable a branch
2. Modify a branch
3. Delete a branch

To view these actions, you will have to click on configure the build link and then click on branch name as shown in below image.

Branch actions in Bamboo

6.12 Configuring build plan permissions

Build plan permissions allow you to assign below permissions to specific user or groups.

1. View build plan
2. Edit build plan
3. Build - right to run the build
4. clone - right to clone the build plan

Below image shows how you can configure the plan permissions. You can also manage
the permissions through global settings on Administration page.

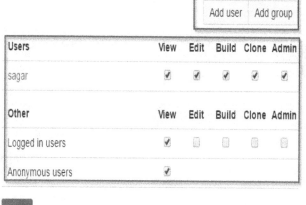

Plan permissions in Bamboo

6.13 Configuring build notifications

We can configure build notification in Bamboo as shown in below images.

On build configuration page, go to Notifications tab. Ensure that you have set up email server or instant messaging server. Click on **Add notification** button.

Adding build notifications in Bamboo

Below image shows that we can add notifications for various types of events like build completion, change of build status, build failures, Job completion etc.

Add a new notification

Add build notification

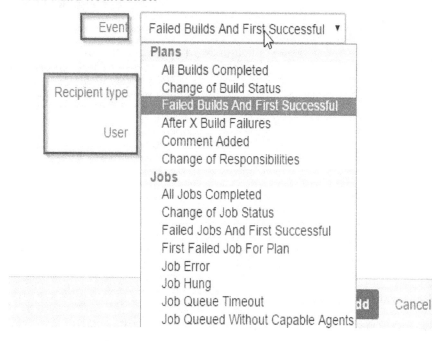

New notification in Bamboo build

6.14 Expiry of the build history

We can manage the build expiry settings at global level as well as at build plan level.

In this topic, we will see how to manage build history clean up settings at build level. You will find Miscellaneous tab in build configuration page as shown in below image. You need to click on override global build expiry configuration.

You can select what items you want to clear as mentioned below.

1. Build results
2. Build artifacts
3. Build logs

We can also specify after how many days the builds should be cleaned.

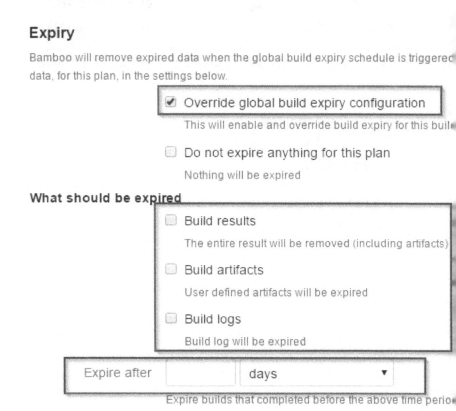

Build history expiry settings in Bamboo

6.15 Passing parameters and variables to the build

We can pass variables to Bamboo build as shown in below image. In Variables tab on build configuration page, you can create new variables. In below image, I have created a variable with name - browser and it's value is chrome.

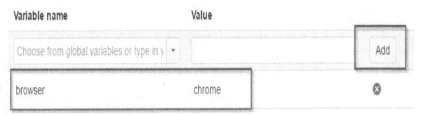

Adding variables to Build in Bamboo

Below image shows how I have passed a variable to task. Note that we can access the variable using below syntax.

${bamboo.variable-name}

Tasks

A task is a piece of work that is being executed as part of the build. The execution of a script, a shell command, an Ant Ta goal are only few examples of Tasks. Learn more about tasks.

You can use runtime, plan and global variables to parameterize your tasks.

1 agent has the capabilitie

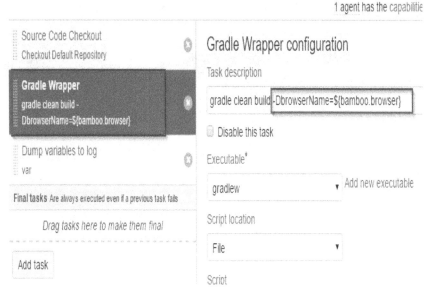

Passing the variable to task in Bamboo

After running the build, at run time the variable is substituted with it's value as shown in below image.

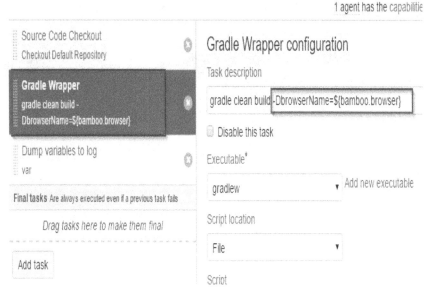

Bamboo variable in build log

7. Java project tasks

7.1 Adding Maven build plan

The important settings of maven task are given below.

1. Provide the path of maven executable
2. Provide any valid maven goal

Below image shows how to configure the maven task in Bamboo. We have set up the clean test goal.

maven task in Bamboo

Below image shows the sample output of the build plan using maven task.

```
build    11-Jun-2016 11:55:17    [INFO]
build    11-Jun-2016 11:55:17    [INFO] --- maven-compiler-plugin:3.1:compile (default-compile) @ testng-artifact ---
build    11-Jun-2016 11:55:21    [INFO] Changes detected - recompiling the module!
build    11-Jun-2016 11:55:21    [INFO] Compiling 1 source file to C:\Users\Sagar\Downloads\atlassian-bamboo-5.12.1\bin\UsersSagarban
build    11-Jun-2016 11:55:26    [INFO]
build    11-Jun-2016 11:55:26    [INFO] --- maven-resources-plugin:2.6:testResources (default-testResources) @ testng-artifact ---
build    11-Jun-2016 11:55:26    [INFO] Using 'UTF-8' encoding to copy filtered resources.
build    11-Jun-2016 11:55:26    [INFO] Copying 1 resource
build    11-Jun-2016 11:55:27    [INFO]
build    11-Jun-2016 11:55:27    [INFO] --- maven-compiler-plugin:3.1:testCompile (default-testCompile) @ testng-artifact ---
build    11-Jun-2016 11:55:27    [INFO] Changes detected - recompiling the module!
build    11-Jun-2016 11:55:27    [INFO] Compiling 1 source file to C:\Users\Sagar\Downloads\atlassian-bamboo-5.12.1\bin\UsersSagarban
classes
build    11-Jun-2016 11:55:27    [INFO]
build    11-Jun-2016 11:55:27    [INFO] --- maven-surefire-plugin:2.19.1:test (default-test) @ testng-artifact ---
build    11-Jun-2016 11:55:29
build    11-Jun-2016 11:55:29    -------------------------------------------------------
build    11-Jun-2016 11:55:29    T E S T S
build    11-Jun-2016 11:55:29    -------------------------------------------------------
build    11-Jun-2016 11:55:30    Running TestSuite
build    11-Jun-2016 11:55:31    ...
build    11-Jun-2016 11:55:31    ... TestNG 6.9.10 by Cédric Beust (cedric@beust.com)
build    11-Jun-2016 11:55:31    ...
build    11-Jun-2016 11:55:31
build    11-Jun-2016 11:55:32    Test1
build    11-Jun-2016 11:55:32    PATH=C:\Program Files\Java\jdk1.8.0_77\bin;C:\ProgramData\Oracle\Java\javapath;C:\Program Files
(x86)\Lenovo\FusionEngine;C:\WINDOWS\system32;C:\WINDOWS;C:\WINDOWS\System32\Wbem;C:\WINDOWS\System32\WindowsPowerShell\v1.0\;C:\Prc
Files\lenovo\easyplussdk\bin;C:\Program Files (x86)\ATI Technologies\ATI.ACE\Core-Static;C:\Program Files (x86)\QuickTime\QTSystem\;
Files\Git\bin;C:\Users\Sagar\AppData\Local\Android\sdk\platform-tools;C:\PROGRA~2\Groovy\GROOVY~1.6\bin;C:\Program Files (x86)\Windc
Live\Shared;C:\WINDOWS\system32\config\systemprofile\.dnx\bin;C:\Program Files\Microsoft DNX\Dnvm\;C:\Program Files\Microsoft SQL
Server\130\Tools\Binn\;C:\Windows\Microsoft.NET\Framework64\v4.0.30319;C:\Program Files (x86)\Microsoft Visual Studio 14.0\Common7\1
2.13\bin;C:\Program Files\Java\jdk1.8.0_77\bin;C:\maven\apache-maven-3.3.9\bin;C:\Windows\Microsoft.NET\Framework64\v4.0.30319;C:\Pr
14.0\Common7\IDE;C:\Users\Sagar\Downloads\gradle-2.13-bin\gradle-2.13\bin
build    11-Jun-2016 11:55:32    BAMBOO_BUILDKEY=MP-TES-JOB1
build    11-Jun-2016 11:55:32    MAVEN2_HOME=C:\maven\apache-maven-3.3.9
build    11-Jun-2016 11:55:32    _RUNJAVA="C:\Program Files\Java\jdk1.8.0_77\jre\bin\java.exe"
build    11-Jun-2016 11:55:32    BAMBOO_CAPABILITY_SYSTEM_BUILDER_MSBUILD_MSBUILD_V2_0__32BIT_=C:\WINDOWS\Microsoft.NET\Framework\v2.
build    11-Jun-2016 11:55:32    SESSIONNAME=Console
build    11-Jun-2016 11:55:32    ALLUSERSPROFILE=C:\ProgramData
```

maven output in Bamboo

7.2 Adding Gradle build plan in Bamboo

By default , there is no support for gradle in the bamboo. You will have to install the groovy tasks for bamboo add-on as stated on **Atlassian** site*(https://bobswift.atlassian.net/wiki/display/BGTP)*

Then follow below steps to add gradle wrapper task.

Gradle wrapper in Bamboo

configuration of gradle wrapper task in Bamboo

```
build    11-Jun-2016 17:52:06   :compileJava UP-TO-DATE
build    11-Jun-2016 17:52:06   :processResources UP-TO-DATE
build    11-Jun-2016 17:52:06   :classes UP-TO-DATE
build    11-Jun-2016 17:52:06   :jar
build    11-Jun-2016 17:52:06   :assemble
build    11-Jun-2016 17:52:11   :compileTestJava
build    11-Jun-2016 17:52:11   :processTestResources UP-TO-DATE
build    11-Jun-2016 17:52:11   :testClasses
build    11-Jun-2016 17:52:18   :test
build    11-Jun-2016 17:52:18
build    11-Jun-2016 17:52:18   categories.SanitySuite > teSanity1 STANDARD_OUT
build    11-Jun-2016 17:52:18       Category X - Running sanity test - 1
build    11-Jun-2016 17:52:18
build    11-Jun-2016 17:52:18   categories.SanitySuite > testSanity2 STANDARD_OUT
build    11-Jun-2016 17:52:18       Category X - Running sanity test - 2
build    11-Jun-2016 17:54:18
build    11-Jun-2016 17:54:18   junit.SimpleSuite > test1 STANDARD_OUT
build    11-Jun-2016 17:54:18       Category Y - executing test1
build    11-Jun-2016 17:54:18
build    11-Jun-2016 17:54:18   junit.SimpleSuite > test2 STANDARD_OUT
build    11-Jun-2016 17:54:18       Category Y - executing test2
build    11-Jun-2016 17:54:19   :check
build    11-Jun-2016 17:54:19   :build
build    11-Jun-2016 17:54:19
build    11-Jun-2016 17:54:19   BUILD SUCCESSFUL
build    11-Jun-2016 17:54:19
build    11-Jun-2016 17:54:19   Total time: 2 mins 53.349 secs
simple   11-Jun-2016 17:54:19   Finished task 'gradle clean build' with result: Success
simple   11-Jun-2016 17:54:19   Running post build plugin 'NCover Results Collector'
simple   11-Jun-2016 17:54:19   Running post build plugin 'Artifact Copier'
simple   11-Jun-2016 17:54:19   Running post build plugin 'npm Cache Cleanup'
simple   11-Jun-2016 17:54:19   Running post build plugin 'Clover Results Collector'
simple   11-Jun-2016 17:54:19   Running post build plugin 'Docker Container Cleanup'
simple   11-Jun-2016 17:54:19   Finalising the build...
simple   11-Jun-2016 17:54:19   Stopping timer.
```

sample gradle output in Bamboo

8. Visual Studio .Net Project tasks

8.1 Adding MSBuild task

MSBuild is used to build .Net project.

MSBuild is used to build the .net project. It generates .dll file for the project. MSBuild task has 2 important settings.

1. executable - MSBuild executable
2. project file - .sln file of .net project

Below images show how to add MSBuild task in Bamboo.

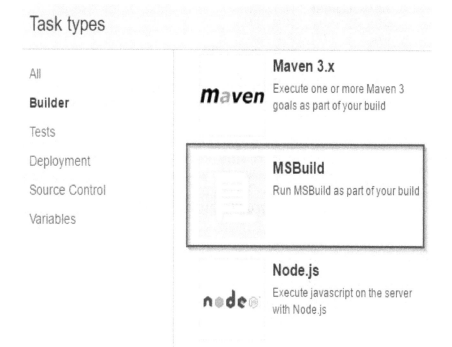

Task types

All		Maven 3.x
Builder	*maven*	Execute one or more Maven 3 goals as part of your build
Tests		
Deployment		**MSBuild**
Source Control		Run MSBuild as part of your build
Variables		
		Node.js
	node	Execute javascript on the server with Node.js

MSBuild task in Bamboo

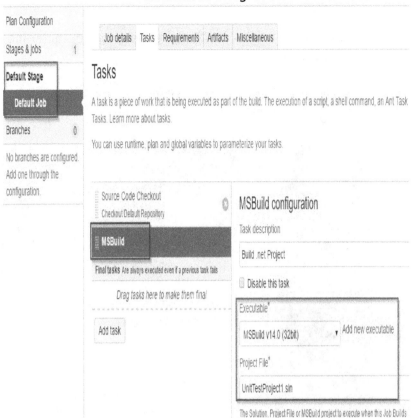

Configure MSBuild in Bamboo

8.2 Adding MSTest task

MSTest is used to execute the tests from the container file in .Net project.

Below images show how to configure the MSTest in Bamboo.

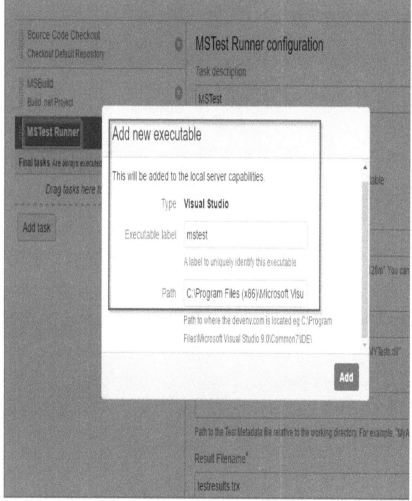

MSTest executable in Bamboo

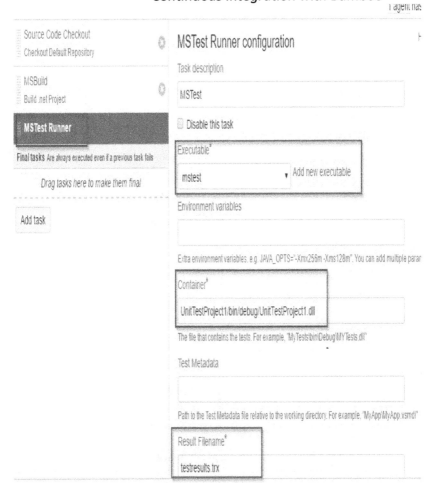

MSTest configuration in Bamboo

Below Image shows the sample MSTest log.

▼ ⊘ Default Job Default Stage

```
11-Jun-2016 13:43:06
11-Jun-2016 13:43:06 Build succeeded.
11-Jun-2016 13:43:06     0 Warning(s)
11-Jun-2016 13:43:06     0 Error(s)
11-Jun-2016 13:43:06
11-Jun-2016 13:43:06 Time Elapsed 00:00:02.45
11-Jun-2016 13:43:10 Microsoft (R) Test Execution Command Line Tool Version 14.0.23107.
11-Jun-2016 13:43:10 Copyright (c) Microsoft Corporation. All rights reserved.
11-Jun-2016 13:43:10
11-Jun-2016 13:43:10 Loading UnitTestProject1/bin/debug/UnitTestProject1.dll...
11-Jun-2016 13:43:11 Starting execution...
11-Jun-2016 13:43:15
11-Jun-2016 13:43:15 Results                 Top Level Tests
11-Jun-2016 13:43:15 -------                 ---------------
11-Jun-2016 13:43:15 Passed                  UnitTestProject1.tests.UnitTest1.TestMethod1
11-Jun-2016 13:43:15 1/1 test(s) Passed
11-Jun-2016 13:43:15
11-Jun-2016 13:43:15 Summary
11-Jun-2016 13:43:15 -------
11-Jun-2016 13:43:15 Test Run Completed.
11-Jun-2016 13:43:15   Passed  1
11-Jun-2016 13:43:15   ---------
11-Jun-2016 13:43:15   Total   1
11-Jun-2016 13:43:15 Results file:  C:\Users\Sagar\Downloads\atlassian-bamboo-5.12.1\bi
11-Jun-2016 13:43:15 Test Settings: Default Test Settings
```

MSTest log in Bamboo

9. Command line builds in Bamboo

9.1 Linux shell build

Linux shell command build can be created by adding the task of type - Script.

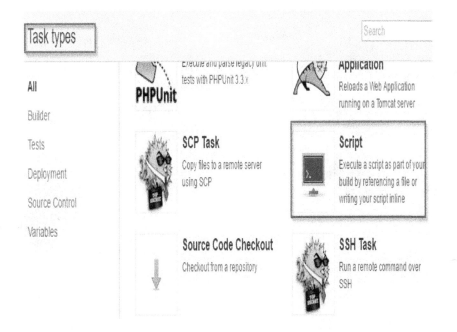

Configuring the Script task

Below image shows how we can configure the script task. Script location can be selected as inline or a file. If we select the inline script location, we need to give the commands to be executed in the script body box.

A task is a piece of work that is being executed as part of the build. The execution of a script, a shel
Tasks. Learn more about tasks.

You can use runtime, plan and global variables to parameterize your tasks.

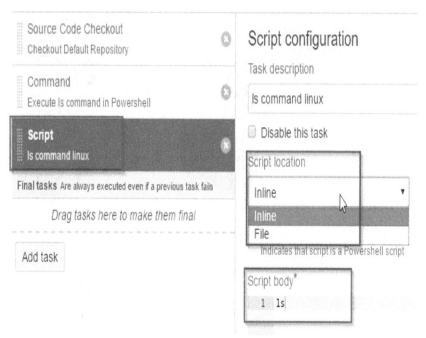

Linux script task configuration in Bamboo

9.2 Windows batch command build

Windows command build can be created by adding the task of type - Script.

Configuring the Script task

Below image shows how we can configure the script task. Script location can be selected as inline or a file. If we select the inline script location, we need to give the commands to be executed in the script body box. In below example - we have executed simple DIR command which displays directories and files in windows.

Tasks

A task is a piece of work that is being executed as part of the build. The execution of a script, a shell Tasks. Learn more about tasks.

You can use runtime, plan and global variables to parameterize your tasks.

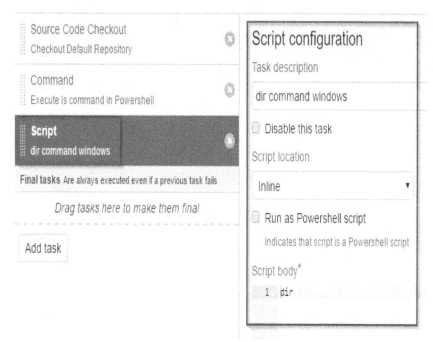

Configuring the windows command task in Bamboo

9.3 Windows Powershell build

Windows Powershell build can be created by adding the
task of type - Script.

Configuring the Script task

Below image shows how we can configure the script task.
Script location can be selected as inline or a file. If we
select the inline script location, we need to give the
commands to be executed in the script body box. In below
example - we have executed simple ls command withing
powershell which displays directories and files in windows.

Notice that we have ticked the checkbox saying **Run as
Powershell script**

A task is a piece of work that is being executed as part of the build. The execution of a script, a shell co Tasks. Learn more about tasks.

You can use runtime, plan and global variables to parameterize your tasks.

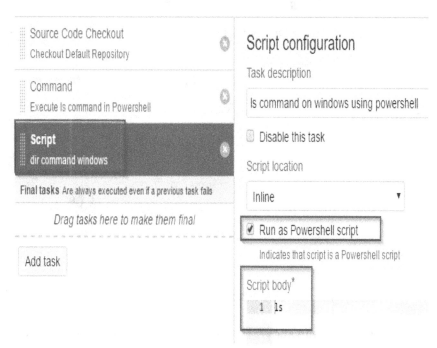

Powershell build in Bamboo

10. Running the build plans manually

We can run any build plan in 2 ways.

1. From the Bamboo Dashboard
2. From the build plan page

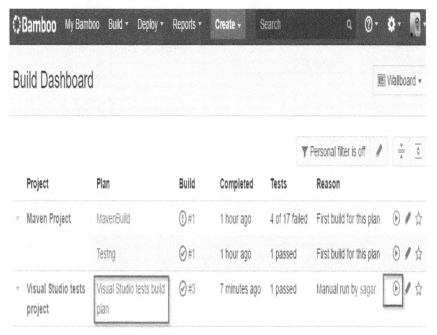

Running build from Dashboard

Running build plan from plan page

11. Viewing the build history and build logs

build history

To view the build history of any plan, click on the name of build plan on the dashboard page and then click on History tab as shown in below image.

From the history tab, we can do below things.

1. View who triggered the build
2. View when the build was triggered
3. View build duration
4. See if there were any tests passed or failed
5. Delete any build run history

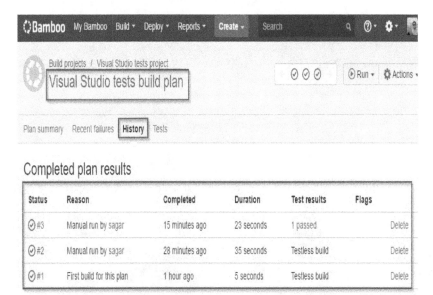

Build history of a build plan in Bamboo

Viewing the build logs

To view the build logs of any build, go to the history of the build.

On build history, you will find all the build runs. Click on the build run which will open build run summary. Then you have to click on the logs tab to view the logs of that specific build.

Below image shows the logs for the build #3 of Visual Studio tests build plan. You can also download the build log or view entire build log as shown in below image.

Viewing the build logs in Bamboo

12. Bamboo Reports

We can generate various reports in Bamboo as mentioned below.

1. Build activity
2. Build duration
3. Build Queued duration
4. Agent Utilization
5. Number of build failures
6. Number of tests
7. % of successful builds
8. % of failed builds

Below images show how to generate above reports.

Custom Reports and Statistics

Compare trends between different plans. You can choose the different reports and

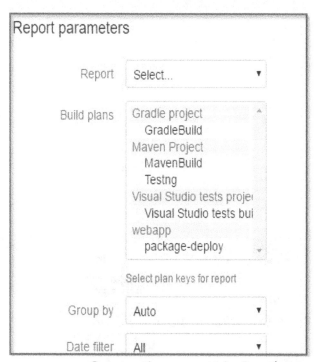

Generating report in Bamboo

Below image shows sample Build duration report in Bamboo.

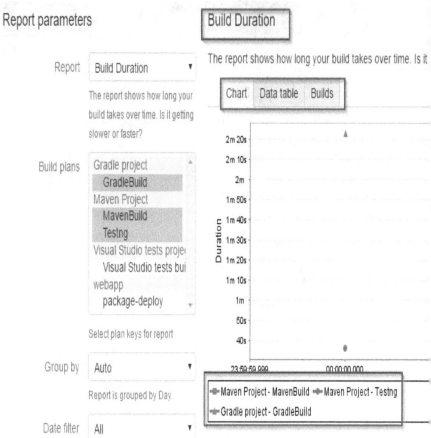

Build Duration Report in Bamboo

13. Authors Page in Bamboo

On Author page, we can see list of all developers who commit to the repositories associated with build plans. For each author, We can see how many builds were triggered, failed, broken and fixed.

Below image shows sample Authors page in Bamboo.

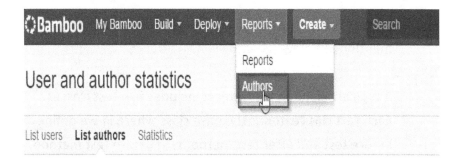

Authors page in Bamboo

14. Executing Selenium tests in Bamboo

In this topic, we are going to look at how we can execute Selenium tests in Bamboo.

I am assuming that you already know how to work with Maven+JUnit, Maven+TestNG, Gradle+JUnit and Gradle+TestNG projects.

In your Selenium project, add few selenium tests as mentioned below.

A typical Selenium test project includes few test classes. Each test class extends the base class where in we define before test and after test methods. In before test method, we create the webdriver instance and also perform test initialization tasks. In after test method, we close the driver and also perform clean up tasks like closing processes created during test run.

Below is the sample base class for all Selenium Test classes.

```
package seleniumtests;


import org.junit.Before;

import org.junit.After;
```

```
import org.openqa.selenium.WebDriver;
import
org.openqa.selenium.firefox.FirefoxDriver;

public class BaseTest
{
    public WebDriver driver;
    @Before
    public void init()
    {
      driver = new FirefoxDriver();
    }
    @After
    public void cleanup()
    {
        driver.close();
        driver.quit();
    }
}
```

Below is the sample test class. In below test class, we have created a simple test to verify the title of website - www.softpost.org

```
package seleniumtests;

import org.junit.Assert;
import org.junit.Test;

public class SmokeTests extends BaseTest
{

    @Test
    public void verifyTitle()
    {
        driver.get("http://www.softpost.org");
```

```
Assert.assertTrue(driver.getTitle().contains("F
ree Software Tutorials"));
    }
}
```

After this, all you need to do is push this project on GitHub or your local repository server.

Then on Bamboo, you need to **create maven build.**

15. Creating and viewing artifacts

Artifacts are nothing but the output of the build. When build finishes the execution, it usually generates some output files. For example - after running testNG tests, report is generated. Bamboo build plan can be configured to store specific artifacts of the build.

Below image shows that we have created one artifact definition wherein all files from build/reports/tests will be copied and saved as artifacts on server.

creating artifact definition in Bamboo

Below image shows how to view the artifacts on server.

Viewing the artifact of the build in Bamboo

Below image shows sample gradle report stored as artifact on the bamboo.

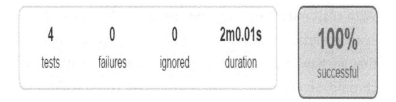

Test Summary

4	0	0	2m0.01s	100% successful
tests	failures	ignored	duration	

Packages Classes

Package	Tests	Failures	Ignored	Duration
categories	2	0	0	0.004s
junit	2	0	0	2m0.01s

gradle report in Bamboo

16. Running customized build plan

When the build is run, it uses the default values for all the variables. But sometimes, we might need to execute the build with different values for the variable.

With customized build run, we can override values of specific variables and run the build. Below image shows that we have a plan variable called as browser with value chrome. So when build will be executed, chrome value will be passed to the build process.

Plan details	Stages	Repositories	Triggers	Branches
Dependencies	Permissions	Notifications	Variables	Miscellaneous
Audit log				

Variables

How to use variables

Variables substitute values in your task configuration and inline scripts. If the key contains the phrase 'password', like 'userpassword' the value will be masked with '**********'

For task configuration fields, use the syntax ${bamboo.myvariablename}. For inline scripts, variables are exposed as shell environment variables which can be accessed using the syntax $bamboo_MY_VARIABLE_NAME (Linux/Mac OS X) or %BAMBOO_MY_VARIABLE_NAME% (Windows).

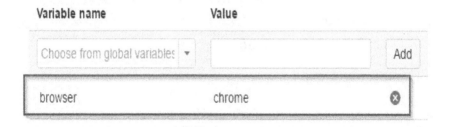

Plan variables in bamboo build

Below image shows how to run the build in customized way.

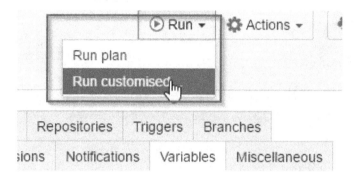

Run customized build in Bamboo

Now let us see how to override the plan variable value. Below image shows that we have overridden browser variable's value as firefox.

Overriding a plan variable in Bamboo

17. Build queue in Bamboo

Build queue shows what all builds are currently running and what all builds are waiting in the queue.

We can also do below things on Build queue page.

1. Recently built builds
2. Stop the builds in queue
3. Reorder the builds in queue

You can view the build queue in Bamboo as shown in below image.

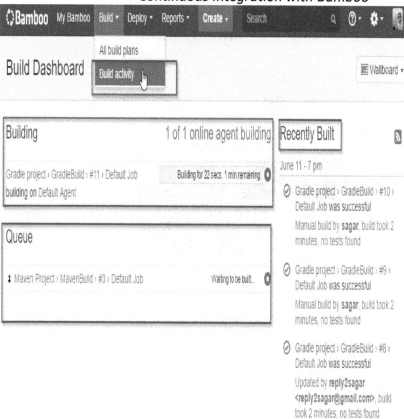

Build queue in Bamboo

18. Bamboo Administration

18.1 Managing build agents

Below image shows how to access Administration page in Bamboo.

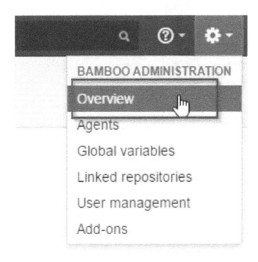

From Bamboo Administration page, you can access Agents page as shown in below image.

Agent page in Bamboo

We can perform below things from Agents page in Bamboo.

1. We can add, edit, delete agents from Administration page.
2. We can also enable/disable agents from Agent page.

To view the information of any agent, click on it. It shows below information.

1. Capabilities - all tools and executables available on this agent are shown here
2. Executable jobs - This tab shows all build plans and jobs that can be executed on this agent.
3. Audit logs - shows when the agent was changed and by whom
4. System errors - shows any errors encountered on the agent

We can also view recent activity of any agent. We can aslo dedicate the agent to specific project or build plan.

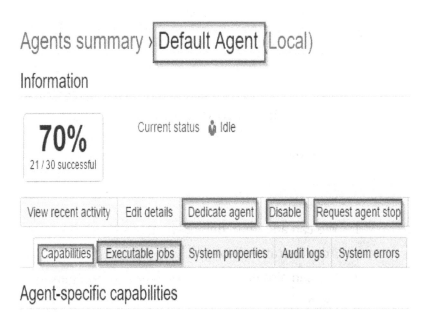

Viewing agent information in Bamboo

Agent matrix allows you to view what all agents can run what all build plans.

18.2 Global Variables

Global variables can be managed from Administration
Page in Bamboo as shown in below image.

We can use global variables while configuring build plans.

Bamboo administration

BUILD RESOURCES

Global variables

Agents

You can use this page to view, add, edit and delete global
build run in Bamboo and can be accessed using ${bambo

Agent matrix

Executables

For task configuration fields, use the syntax ${bamboo.m}
exposed as shell environment variables which can be acc
$bamboo_MY_VARIABLE_NAME (Linux/Mac OS X) or %E

JDKs

Server capabilities

Variable name	Value
ToolPath	xyz

Global variables

Linked repositories

Shared credentials

Repository settings

Global Variables in Bamboo

18.3 User Management

From user management page, you can do below things

1. Create new user
2. View all users
3. Edit any of the user
4. Add or remove the user from specific group when editing the user
5. Search for user

Below image shows how we can manage users in Bamboo from Administration Page.

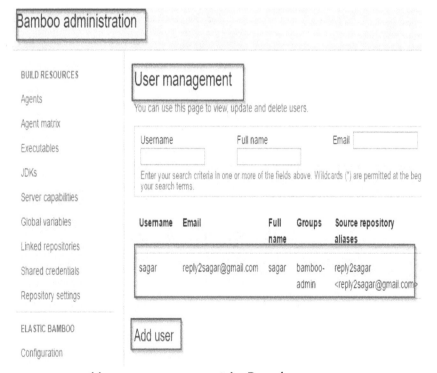

User management in Bamboo

18.4 Server Capabilities

Server capabilities are nothing but the executable tools available on Bamboo.

This page allows you to view, add, edit and delete executable tools on server like maven, gradle, git etc.

Server Capabilities in Bamboo

18.5 Linked Repositories

You can manage all linked repositories in Bamboo from Administration page as shown in below image.

You can add, edit, delete the repositories from this page.

Bamboo Repositories

18.6 Group Management

From Group management page, you can do below things

1. Create new group
2. View all groups
3. Edit any of the Group
4. Delete group

Below image shows how you can manage groups in Bamboo.

Managing groups in Bamboo

18.7 Global Permissions

From Global Permissions page, we can manage below things in Bamboo.

1. who can access Bamboo
2. Who can create build plans
3. Who are admins

Below image shows how we can manage global

Global permissions

You can edit your global application level permissions here. Permissions can be granted to specific users or groups. Please note these are global application permissions. For plan level permissions, please go to the plan configuration page.

Groups	Access	Create plan	Create repository	Admin
bamboo-admin	✓	✓	✓	✓

Other	Access	Create plan	Create repository	Admin
All logged in users	✓	✗	✗	
Anonymous users	✓			

Edit

Global permissions in Bamboo

18.8 Add-ons Management

From Add-on section, you can do below things.

1. Install new add-ons
2. Uninstall existing add-ons
3. Upload Add on
4. Update existing add-ons
5. Enable or disable add-ons

Below image shows how you can manage Add-ons in Bamboo.

Managing Add-ons in Bamboo

18.9 Email and IM server

In Bamboo, you can configure the Mail and IM server settings (from Administration Page) so that notification mails are sent whenever the build fails or passes.

On Email server settings, we can configure below settings.

1. Email address, name, prefix to be used to sent out mail notification
2. Email server name, port, protocol

From IM page, you can configure IM server settings (e.g. Jabber IM).

Below image shows how you can configure Email and Instant Messenger.

Configure mail server details

Configure mail server details

What email settings should Bamboo use?. Please enter either a SMTP server hostname, or the JI of a javax.mail.Session object to use.

Name*	Bamboo

Provide a name for this email server (this will be displayed on notification emails).

From address*	

This is the email address Bamboo-generated emails are sent from.

Subject prefix	[Bamboo]

This is the tag added to the start of the subject line to identify Bamboo-generated email. [Bamboo].

☐ Exclude email header "precedence: bulk"

Email settings	SMTP ▼

Choose either a SMTP server or a JNDI location

SMTP server*	

Email server settings in Bamboo

18.10 Changing the default port

In this post, let us see how to change the port and IP address of Bamboo server.

You can access port and IP address settings from General Configuration section in Administration page as shown in below image.

General configuration

You may change the following Bamboo configuration properties.

What is the title of this Bamboo instance?

Name* | Atlassian Bamboo

The name of this Bamboo instance.

What is the server's address?

Base URL* | http://192.168.56.1:9999

This is the base URL of this installation of Bamboo. All links created (for emails etc) by This URL.

for example "http://192.168.56.1:9999"

Broker configuration

Broker URL | tcp://0.0.0.0:54663?wireFormat.maxInactivityDuration=300000

Requires Bamboo restart after changing.

Server address in Bamboo

10.11 License Information

You can view the license information of Bamboo in License section in Administration page as shown in below image.

License page shows below details.

1. Organisation
2. Date purchased
3. License Type
4. Number of local agents supported
5. Number of remote agents supported
6. License Expiry date
7. Server Id

License key details

Existing license key details

You may view your licensing details or use the update license form to update the li with.

Organisation	sagarsalunke
Date purchased	11 June 2016

License type	Bamboo (Server) 250 Remote Agents: Evaluation License
Number of local agents supported	Unlimited
Number of remote agents supported	250
License expiry date	11 July 2016
Server id	BDOC-2HHU-OM64-PHMP
Support entitlement number (sen)	SEN-L8030751

License information in Bamboo

18.12 Bamboo System Information

Bamboo system information can be viewed from System Information section in Administration page of Bamboo.

Below types of system information is shown in Bamboo.

1. System properties
2. Java tools
3. All environment variables
4. Memory details
5. Bamboo Paths
6. Plug-ins installed

Below image shows sample system information of a Bamboo server.

Bamboo administration

BUILD RESOURCES

Agents

Agent matrix

Executables

JDKs

Server capabilities

Global variables

Linked repositories

Shared credentials

Repository settings

ELASTIC BAMBOO

Configuration

System information

System properties

System date	Friday, 24 Jun 2016
System time	18:50:42
Up time	18 minutes, 51 seconds (since Fri Jun 24 18:31:50
Username	Sagar
User timezone	Australia/Brisbane
User locale	English (India)
System encoding	Cp1252
Operating system	Windows 10 10.0
Operating system architecture	amd64
Available	4

System information in Bamboo

18.13 Bamboo Audit log

Audit log shows all the activities done on Bamboo server like creation of plan, adding global variables, Adding or removing build agents.

You can view audit log from Administration page in Bamboo as shown in below image.

		Disable audit logging	Delete all global audit logs	Delete all audit logs

Global configuration change history

Timestamp	User	Changed field	Old value	New value
20:22, 23 Jun	sagar	Variable [ToolPath] has been created.		xyz
09:05, 12 Jun	sagar	New Plan created		WEB-PAC
09:04, 12 Jun	sagar	Global repository webapp has been created.		
19:45, 11 Jun	sagar	New Plan branch created		VST-VST1
19:43, 11 Jun	sagar	Plan deleted: Visual Studio tests project - Visual Studio tests build plan - bugfix (VST-VST0)		
19:40, 11 Jun	sagar	New Plan branch created		VST-VST0
17:47, 11 Jun	sagar	Server Capability added		system.builder.gradle

Audit log in Bamboo

18.14 Import/Export build plans

By default, Bamboo exports only build plan configuration. But you can choose if you want to export results, artifacts and build logs by selecting the check boxes on export page as shown in below image.

Export

ⓘ Bamboo will be unavailable until the export process completes.

Specify export paths

Depending on the number of builds and tests, the export may take a long time to complete and may requ
large amounts of disk space. Please make sure you have enough disk space before proceeding.

Export directory path	**C:\Users\Sagar\Downloads\atlassian-bamboo-5.12.1\bin\Users Sagar bamboo home\exports**
File name	export_atlassianbamboo_51211_20160624.zip

Specify the file name for Bamboo export

☑ Export results

Uncheck this box if you only want to export the plan configuration

☐ Export artifacts

Should Bamboo export build artifacts

☑ Export build logs

Should Bamboo export build logs

Export

Export builds in Bamboo

You can import the build plans by providing the path of exported file as shown in below image. Before importing, you can tack a back up by selecting the Back up data checkbox but that's optional.

⚠ You need an administration login in the import file to be able to make changes after import.

Specify import paths

The import process will delete this instance and restore data from a previous export of Bamboo. This includes login data hence you will need an administration login that is contained in the Bamboo data to be imported. Bamboo will be unavailable until the import process is complete which may take some time. Please check the paths of your executables and JDK after importing.

File path

Specify the absolute path to the file on the server from which Bamboo is to import from. For example "C:\Users\Sagar\Downloads\atlassian-bamboo-5.12.1\bin\UsersSagarbamboo-home\export.zip".

☑ Backup data?

Although this will make the import process longer, backup is strongly recommended. Import will not proceed unless Bamboo successfully backs up.

Import the builds in Bamboo

18.15 Build History clean up

From Expiry section in Administration page, we can specify when the build history should be cleared as shown in below image.

As shown in image, we can select what data to be deleted

1. Complete build results, artifacts and logs
2. Build and release artifacts only
3. Build and deployment logs only

We can also set the duration after which all builds will be cleaned.

Configure when builds and releases get removed from your Bamboo instance automatically, to keep overall file size under control and clean up the user interface. Individual plans can override global settings. Learn more about build and release expiry.

Global expiry configuration

Bamboo will remove expired data based on the settings below. This global configuration can be overridden for individual plan by updating the Post Actions for a plan. Refer to the documentation for help configuring the settings below.

Removal schedule

Bamboo will check for expired data using the global and plan override expiry configurations at intervals based on the cron expression defined below.

Build clean up in Bamboo

18.16 Bulk edit plan permissions

You can edit the plan permissions of a given user from Administration page as shown in below image.

There are 5 types of permissions that you can assign to any specific user.

1. View plan
2. Edit plan
3. Build plan (Execute plan)
4. Clone plan
5. Admin

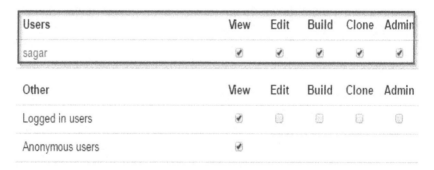

Bulk edit plan permissions wizard

Users	View	Edit	Build	Clone	Admin
sagar	☑	☑	☑	☑	☑

Other	View	Edit	Build	Clone	Admin
Logged in users	☑	☐	☐	☐	☐
Anonymous users	☑				

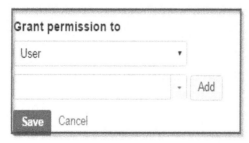

Bulk edit plan permissions in Bamboo

18.17 Move build plan

You can move plans from one project to another project from Move plans section in Administration page as shown in below image.

You will need to provide the name of new project. Then you can select the plans that you want to move to new project. Please note that you can also move plan to existing project as well.

You can move a plan to another project with this wizard. Simply select
As names and keys may conflict, you'll then be asked to enter new nar
changing plan keys, this operation requires some slow operations (e.g.

Destination project	New Project ▼
	The project you want to move your plans to
Project name*	
Project key*	

Eg. AT (for a project named Atlassian)

Select: All, None

Gradle project

☑ GradleBuild

Maven Project

☑ MavenBuild

☐ Testng

Visual Studio tests project

☐ Visual Studio tests build plan

webapp

☐ package-deploy

Move

Moving build plans to different project in Bamboo

18.18 Delete build plans Bulk actions

Delete build

Now let us see how to delete build plans in Bamboo.

You can delete plans from Administration page - Remove plan section as shown in below image. Notice that you can select multiple build plans and delete them at once.

Remove plans

Check the plans to be removed

Check one or more of the following plans to be deleted:

Select: All, None

Gradle project

☐ GradleBuild

☐ **Maven Project**

☐ MavenBuild

☐ Testng

☐ **Visual Studio tests project**

☐ Visual Studio tests build plan

☐ **webapp**

☐ package-deploy

Delete

Delete build plans in Bamboo

Bulk actions

We can do below bulk actions from Administration page in Bamboo.

1. Enabling and disabling plans
2. Removing all notifications
3. Updating VCS repositories
4. Replacing triggers
5. Running manual builds

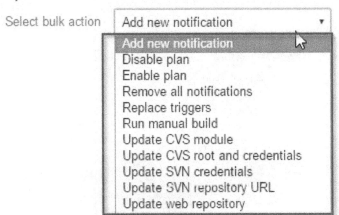

Bulk actions in Bamboo

19. Adding deployment project to build plan

We can easily associate the deployment project with build plan in Bamboo.

Please follow below steps to create deployment project.

Before creating the deployment project for any build plan, ensure that artifacts generated by the build plan are shared as shown in below image.

Edit artifact definition

Name* VSTest Report

If the artifact is shared, the name must be unique within the plan

Location

Specify the directory (relative path) to find your artifact. e.g. *target*

Copy pattern* testresults.trx

Specify the name (or Ant file copy pattern) of the artifact(s) you want to keep. e.g. ***/*.jar*

☑ Shared

Make the artifact available to be used in other builds and deployments.

Ensure that artifacts are shared

To create new deployment project, configure the plan and go to the stages tab. Then click on Create deployment project.

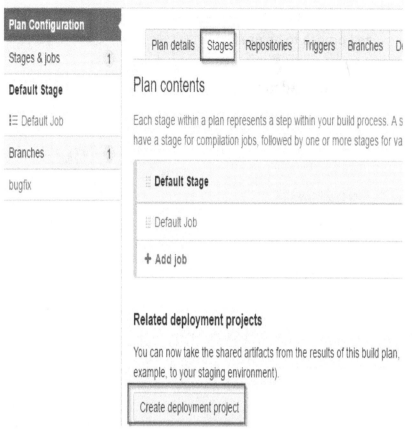

Create deployment project in Bamboo

On next page, you need to provide the name of the project and branch to be used.

Deployment project details

Name* | Deployment for Visual Studio tests prc

Description |

Link to build plan

Shared artifacts of the selected plan will be bundled into releases. Releases will be deployed to the environments.

Build plan* | Visual Studio tests project › Visual Studio tests build plan ▾

Start typing the plan name or use the down arrow to select a plan. The selected plan will be used as the sour a release.

◉ Use the main plan branch

Currently ᚴ master

◎ Use a custom plan branch

[Create deployment project] Cancel

Deployment project name and branch in Bamboo

On next page, you need to provide the environment where the deployment should be made.

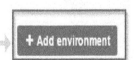

Deployment projects / Deployment for Visual Studio tests project

Configuration: Deployment for Visual Studio tests project

What you want to deploy

Source build plan Visual Studio tests project › Visual Studio tests build plan

Available artifacts VSTest Report

Edit build plan   Release versioning   Project permissions

+ Add environment

Adding environment for deployment in Bamboo

On next page, provide the name of environment and continue to task setup.

Set up environment for Deployment for Visual Studio tests project

Environments represent where releases are deployed to.

Environment details

Environment name* | QA

e.g. Staging, QA, or Production

Description | Testing environment

Continue to task setup | Create and back | Cancel

Environment name for deployment in Bamboo

On next page, you can add one or more deployment tasks.

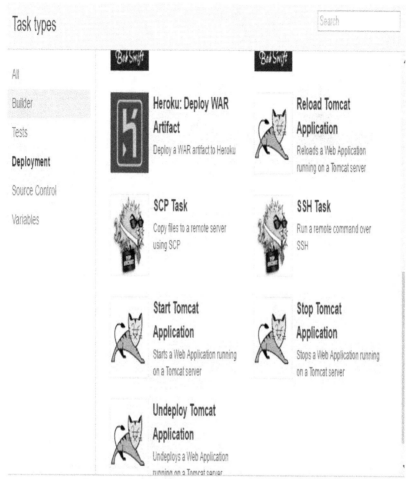

Deployment tasks in Bamboo

Below image shows that we have added SCP task to transfer the artifact on FTP server.

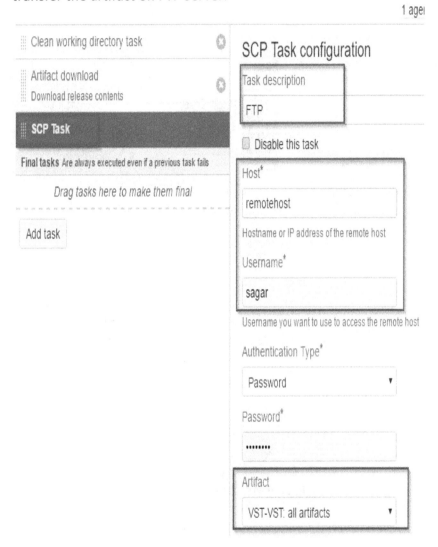

SCP deployment task in Bamboo

You can view all deployment projects in Bamboo as shown in below image. To start the deployment, you need to click on arrow-cloud icon.

Viewing all deployment projects in Bamboo

On next page, you can select the build result and also provide the release name.

Deployment preview: QA

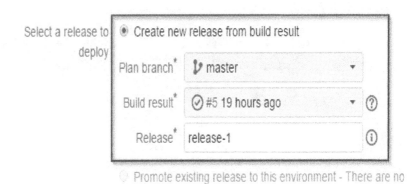

Start deployment in Bamboo

20. Web application deployment to tomcat using Bamboo

In this article, we are going to take a look at how to deploy war file to Tomcat using Bamboo.

Here is the list of steps you need to follow.

1. Create a new build plan which will checkout the source code of web application from repository.
2. Use maven or gradle task to build and package the application. This will create the .war file in output directory.
3. Create a artifact definition to copy this war file and save on the server. Ensure that this artifact is shared.
4. Create a deployment project for this build plan.
5. Add tomcat deployment task to deploy the .war file

Below images will guide you through the entire process.

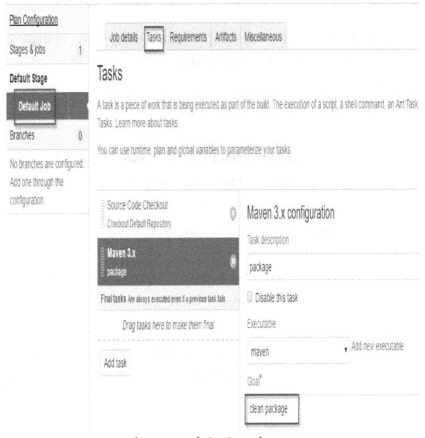

maven package task in Bamboo

Edit artifact definition

Name* | war

If the artifact is shared, the name must be unique within the plan

Location | target

Specify the directory (relative path) to find your artifact. e.g. *target*

Copy pattern* | mywebapp.war

Specify the name (or Ant file copy pattern) of the artifact(s) you want to keep. e.g. **/*.jar*

☑ Shared

Make the artifact available to be used in other builds and deployments.

war artifact in Bamboo

Then you have to create a new deployment project for this build. You will find the button to create new deployment project in build plan configuration -> Stages tab.

Deploy tomcat application task in Bamboo

Below image shows how to configure the Deploy Tomcat Application task.

You need to provide below settings.

1. Tomcat Manager url - By default it is http://localhost:8080/manager
2. You need to also provide the username and password for tomcat manager
3. Finally you have to give application context path

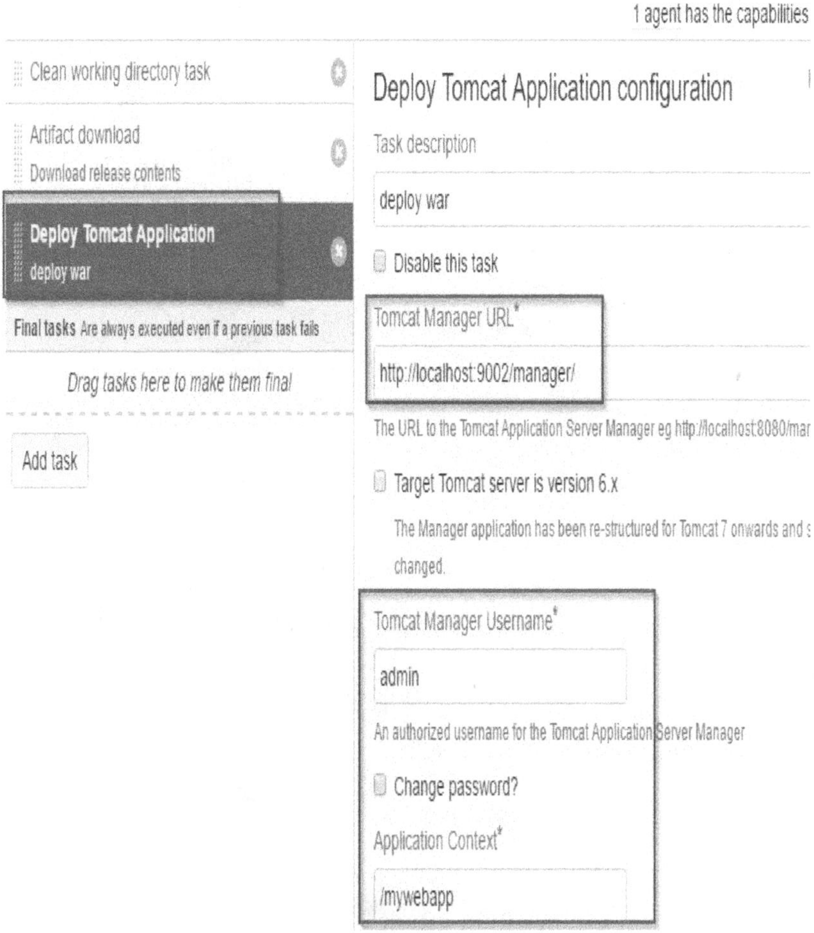

Deploy tomcat application task configuration in Bamboo

www.ingramcontent.com/pod-product-compliance
Lightning Source LLC
Chambersburg PA
CBHW071221050326
40689CB00011B/2393